A MUCH-ABUSED LETTER

A MUCH-ABUSED LETTER

BY

GEORGE TYRRELL

AUTHOR OF "LEX CREDENDI," ETC.

> Ay me! what act
> That roars so loud and thunders in the index?
> *Hamlet*

WIPF & STOCK · Eugene, Oregon

Wipf and Stock Publishers
199 W 8th Ave, Suite 3
Eugene, OR 97401

A Much Abused Letter
By Tyrrell, George, SJ
ISBN 13: 978-1-62032-347-2
Publication date 7/15/2012
Previously published by Longmans, Green and Co, 1906

CONTENTS

	PAGE
INTRODUCTION	1
LETTER TO A UNIVERSITY PROFESSOR	37
NOTES	91
EPILOGUE	101

A MUCH-ABUSED LETTER

INTRODUCTION

IT is necessary to justify the present publication of a letter whose privacy was originally its chief justification. To do so I need only retrace briefly the steps by which I have arrived at a decision counter to my first intention.

On 7 January, 1906, I received a letter from the late Father Martin, General of the Jesuits, in which he says: "My only motive in writing is to learn from your Reverence whether or not you are the author of the expressions quoted in the Milanese 'Corriere della Sera' of 1 January, of which I send you a copy herewith. The Archbishop of Milan asks me whether it is true that any Father of the Society has written such things, and I want an answer from you which I can transmit to the Archbishop."

The following is a translation of the enclosure:

THE IDEAS OF A CATHOLIC REFORMER
(AN UNPUBLISHED BROCHURE)
(From our Vatican Correspondent)

ROME, *December* 31. P.M.

I have come across a most interesting document with which I make haste to acquaint you. It is a brochure entitled, "A Confidential Letter to a Friend who is a Professor of Anthropology." The origin of this document—not on sale, and in possession of but few—is as follows: An eminent English Catholic,[1] finding it impossible to square his science with his faith, had resolved to give up Catholicism, and had revealed his intention to a friend of his who is an English Jesuit. The latter sought to dissuade him, and to that end addressed to him the Confidential Letter now in my hands. In point of boldness, the ideas of this Jesuit go beyond anything so far published by even the most advanced "reformist" Catholics. I wish I could reproduce this strange document in its entirety, which reads like a page from Fogazzaro's "Santo"; but I must confine myself to the pith of the matter.

[1] This account abounds in minor inaccuracies.

"To-day," writes the English Jesuit,[1] "the positions of conservative Catholics can only be maintained by force of systematic or wilful ignorance. I see how the vigorous historical investigation of the origin and development of Christianity must undermine many of our most fundamental assumptions in regard to dogmas and institutions. I see how the sphere of the miraculous is daily limited by the growing difficulty in verifying such facts, and the growing facility of reducing either them or the belief in them to natural and recognized causes. I see and feel moreover how these and like objections would be as nothing could we point triumphantly to the Christian ethos of the Church, to the religious spirit developed by her system as by no other; and were there not in the approved writings of her ascetical teachers, and her moralists; in the prevailing practices of her confessors and directors; in the liturgical biographies of her canonized saints; in the principles of her government and in her methods of education; much that revolts the very same moral and religious sense to which in the first

[1] I re-translate from the Italian translation so as to reproduce one or two inaccuracies which are of moment.

instance her claims to our submission must appeal. Here indeed, as you say, we are involved seemingly in self-contradiction; as soon, namely, as authority bids us repudiate the very principles and sentiments on which alone our obedience to it can rest."

Nevertheless, the author of the Confidential Letter, while recognizing these grave defects of traditional Catholicism, dissuades his friend from leaving the Church.

"Catholicism is not primarily a theology, or at most a system of practical observances regulated by that theology. No, Catholicism is primarily a life, and the Church a spiritual organism in whose life we participate, and theology is but an attempt of that life to formulate and understand itself—an attempt which may fail wholly or in part without affecting the value and reality of the said life."

In fine, the author develops at great length the notion that official and theoretical Catholicism is only approximatively representative of living Catholicism; and he applies to the question of faith the now generally familiar distinction between the conscious and the subconscious. "How little do we know of our own deepest sentiments; of what we believe underneath our surface beliefs; of our hidden capacities of good or evil!"[1]

"It is the function of a good representative government to formulate the thoughts, wishes, and sentiments of the people. But how rarely does this obtain! So with the Church.

"The truths which regulate our spiritual life are but few, and are too fundamental to be dependent on the fate of any particular theological school. Thus in the lives of the greater saints, that which lends them their Christian and Catholic character has but little relation to the complications of theological instruction. The whole of the Christian and Catholic creed should be viewed as a symbol of the impress made by the Infinite on the understanding of a great and eminent fraction of the human race. For the most part the theologians, fallible and ignorant mortals like the rest of us, are in good faith, as were some of those strict-minded rabbis who refused to listen to Christ, who condemned His teaching as heretical, who quoted

[1] What follows is a rather curious patchwork of passages from different pages of the letter fastened together by a few sentences of which I cannot claim the authorship. Still, I do not quarrel with the result.

the prophets to show that salvation was of the Jews alone, and that in the end the whole world would be circumcised. How right they were, and yet how wrong! Well, may not this history repeat itself? May not our theologians be right, but in another sense than they imagine? May not Catholicism, like Judaism, be destined to a far higher and nobler form of life than any hitherto attained? Catholicism, the author concludes, remains the highest expression, the most efficacious instrument of the spiritual life so long as it is not robbed of its liberty or tied to a faction."

This Letter, of which I have been able to give but a feeble analysis, and which will surely be published sooner or later, strikes me as an important document, and makes one of the strangest pages in the history of the Catholic Reform Movement. It sounds, I repeat, like a chapter of "Il Santo," and will no doubt interest the numerous readers of Fogazzaro.

In reply to the Father General's letter, I wrote (13 January) as follows:—

"I hasten to acknowledge as much responsibility as I honestly can for the 'Lettera Confidenziale.' I do not know[1] who has translated it, nor have I read the translation. I am told it has been freely adapted to suit local exigencies, and for these adaptations of course I cannot answer. But I have no doubt that the substance of it—all that you would most dislike—is founded on a letter written by me two or three years ago to meet a particular yet not uncommon case. There is no statement of that original Letter which is not theologically defensible. Yet as a whole it is a medicine for extreme cases; not for common ailments. It can only be judged as a whole, in the context of its suppositions, and not by mischievous and sensational extracts. It supposes explicitly that things are as bad, not as the writer but, as the recipient imagines. You cannot but know that thousands of educated Catholics who are not experts in criticism or history, are aware of the disputes of experts about the most fundamental matters, and that the mere existence of such disputes reduces them to a state of perfectly inculpable theological confusion which they easily mistake for loss of faith. I myself am no expert, and am in the same position as they; and I am

[1] I did not then.

bound in conscience to share with my fellow-sufferers those considerations which enable me to cling to the Church with implicit faith in spite of temporary theological obscurities. Were every one to leave the Church who is unable to arbitrate between contending critics, who could be saved? The remedy for the "inexpert" is prayer, patience, and work; not controversy. What would really do harm would be the publicity and notoriety given to such a Letter by any kind of official notice of it. Till —— was condemned, he was comparatively unknown, and his dry technical writings were read mostly by those already in sympathy with them. But now he has become a cult and a fashion, and for ten who followed him before, a thousand follow, or profess to follow, him now. The methods of one time are not always the best for another time."

In reply to this, His Paternity wrote (20 January) insisting anew on the scandal caused by those extracts from the "Letter," which were published in the "Corriere della Sera." "And although," he continues, "you say it was a private letter written a good while ago and adapted to the peculiar mental requirements of the receiver, yet, according to the opinion of learned theologians whose judgment I have consulted, it certainly contains many inadmissible assertions, and what is still more certain, it has caused scandal to many, even to some eminent dignitaries who reasonably complain that the Society should allow such things to be written by her subjects. I am therefore obliged to remove this scandal, and to require you to send me a declaration, to be published in the papers, repudiating such doctrines as are there[1] propounded."

In reply to this point of His Paternity's letter, I wrote (24 January):—

"As to the 'Lettera Confidenziale,' it is hardly worth while offering an explanation which falls so short of your requirements. Still, it would be unjust not to exonerate the Society from all responsibility. But you would not, I am sure, wish me to repudiate what I should not have written had I not sincerely believed it. Am I to deny, or pretend to deny, the existence of the common difficulties enumerated in the

[1] Sc. in the "Corriere's" quotations.

first paragraph quoted by the 'Corriere'? Have not the authorities themselves admitted all these things? Am I to say that Religion *is* primarily theology, and *not* Eternal Life? Am I to say that Catholicism is *not* something greater and grander than can ever attain adequate expression in its theology or in its institutions, however they may progress? I should be contradicting the Scriptures and the greatest saints and doctors of the Church."

The "explanation" which I enclosed for publication ran as follows:—

"Sir,—I have been ordered by those who have a right to command me to explain my position in regard to the 'Lettera Confidenziale,' noticed in the 'Corriere della Sera' of 1 January, 1906. Let me say first that I am not responsible for the adaptations and changes of the Italian translation, which I have not read, and whose author I do not know. The original letter was perfectly private—an *argumentum ad hominem*, adapted throughout to the presuppositions of the recipient, not to those of the writer. Those presuppositions, owing to the publicly notorious disputes of experts about fundamental matters, are common to thousands of sincerely religious educated laymen who are *not* experts in criticism and theology, and whose position is simply one of 'inculpable ignorance.' If all such were allowed to mistake theological confusion for loss of faith, the Church would lose many of her most living members. It is needful, therefore, to remind them that in such states of blameless perplexity the implicit faith of the little child suffices. To publish such a letter broadcast would be to administer to all the medicine intended only for some. That the 'Corriere' should have made part of it public was certainly not my wish, nor probably that of the translator. As they appear, isolated from their context and presuppositions, the paragraphs may seem startling and sensational. Yet read carefully they contain nothing that has not been said over and over again by saints and doctors of the Church. Only the first sentence misrepresents my meaning. It puts *voluntaria* for *involuntaria*, and applies to 'le posizioni dei catholici conservatori' in general what I said only of certain particular conservative positions in Scripture criticism abandoned now by the more moderate conservatives, and maintained only by those who do not, or will not, read. Needless to say that the Society of Jesus is in no way responsible for private correspondences and conversations never destined for publicity, and therefore never submitted to its official censorship. I am, etc."

On 7 February the English Provincial of the Society notified to me that "the document from Rome severing my connexion with the Society had come."

Before accepting it, and as a check on such possible misstatements as have actually been made, I wrote to ask precisely on what ground I was dismissed. The General replied to the Provincial, quoting his own letter to me dated 1 February, which, being enclosed with the form of dismissal, I had not yet received:—

"The reason of the dismissal is clearly indicated in my letter to Father Tyrrell of 1 February, namely: 'Which defence,[1] as it fails to remove the scandal, does not satisfy the demands of ecclesiastical authority nor of the Society. And since your Reverence declares

[1] Against the complaints raised by the passages published in the "Corriere."

that he cannot send such a declaration as is required, nothing remains, etc.'"[1]

Although it may not be strictly relevant, I may as well add here the note (19 February) by which I closed this correspondence, and which

[1] I wish to note here that it was not the Letter as a whole, but strictly and only the passages quoted in the "Corriere" which I was required to repudiate. Other parts of the Letter I could have repudiated more easily; for even if absolutely defensible, their first sense is obviously counter to received theology. But journalists are not theologians, and easily mistake commonplaces in smart clothes for sensational novelties. Indeed, ecclesiastical authorities themselves will sooner tolerate modernity in the garb of antiquity than antiquity tricked out in the newest fashion, and this because "the faithful," like any other public, is influenced by sound rather than sense. Thus only can I explain the scandal said to be given to certain grave Church dignitaries by what is surely as banal in substance as anything I have ever written; and that is saying much. No doubt the "Corriere's" unfortunate mistranslation, or misprint, of the first line was not calculated to prepossess the said dignitaries in favour of the remainder, read in the lurid light of so ungracious an insinuation. But having corrected that error, I could not, on reading and re-reading the passages many times, find aught to amend or repudiate. An authoritative judgment of a Sacred Congregation would of course have required some act of at least external deference on my part; but here it was a question of repudiation, of deposing my opinion in favour of another, and this in deference to the judgment of certain anonymous theologians who neither stated their precise points of dissent nor the reasons which might have brought me round to their view; who told me that I was wrong, but did not say where or why.

testifies to my sentiments of respect for the late General :—

"Your Paternity,—I should like to assure you, now that I stand outside the Society, how completely I realize that we have both of us been driven to this unpleasant issue by the necessities of our several minds and consciences, and your Paternity still more by the exigencies of a most difficult position. You may depend on me that whatever explanations I may at any time be forced to give of what has happened will make this quite apparent. Nothing could be further from my sentiments than any kind of personal rancour or resentment. I feel that this is a collision of systems and tendencies rather than of persons, and that many such collisions must occur before the truth of both sides meets in some higher truth. And though you may say, God forbid! I do not doubt that in the deepest principle of all we are more in agreement with one another than with many of our respective fellow-thinkers. I thank you for your promised prayers and holy sacrifices. My own sacrifices must now be of another—and more expensive if less valuable —sort,[1] but such as they are I will offer them for you."

[1] Alluding to the suspension entailed in my dismissal.

Even had the confidence expressed in this letter been mistaken, I should not regret having written it or having erred on that side rather than the other. But those later untoward developments, which at first sight seem to convict me of too easy a trustfulness, admit of another explanation; and I still believe that Father Martin acted against me always with reluctance, and only in obedience to pressure brought to bear upon him by others; nay, that he even restrained the more intemperate zeal of those whom his last illness and death left free to follow their bent unchecked.

Although the Confidential Letter was not immediately put on the Index—probably for the reasons suggested above in my letter of 13 January—yet other circumstances, into which I need not enter, soon lent it as great a notoriety as such an official condemnation would have done.

Moreover, at Rome, where controversial temperance is difficult and perhaps impossible, the Letter came into prominence just when a storm had been long brewing, and therefore drew to itself all the reactionary electricity with which the air was then charged. Even "Il

Santo" seemed more forgivable. The "Corriere's" estimate of its unique and unparalleled boldness became an article of faith with multitudes to whom it was inaccessible because unpublished, and it was accepted as fixing the high-water mark of liberal Catholic advance.

To the few who had read the Letter for themselves, and in general to the narrow circle of my more intimate friends, these sensational reports of its character were of as little consequence as to myself. But on the larger and more indefinite multitude of those who had got to know me and trust me through my writings alone, the effect was necessarily "scandalous," i.e. spiritually harmful, in one or other of two ways. Either their confidence in me, and therefore in all the good they had seemed to derive from me, was rudely shaken; or else their confidence in those authorities who had condemned me, i.e. in their normal ex-officio spiritual guides.

To my less intimate friends and well-wishers, therefore, I owe a strict debt of explanation. It is not merely that as a man I have an inalienable right to defend my good name, but that the said right can and has become a clear duty from which no one on earth can dispense me. The many Catholics of the reactionary school who have long, and in a sense rightly, distrusted me and my spirit and method may well be pardoned if they use this *dénouement* to point a moral and adorn a tale. Grace might seal their lips, but Nature is not equal to such miracles of generosity. They will not be inclined to minimize the theological trespasses of the "Confidential Letter," especially where exaggeration is safe from the possible check of reference. Anything may be true of a letter which nobody can see. Hence, those who have trusted me are put to confusion and are at a loss what to think or say. In every hypothesis I am bound to give them the chance of seeing for themselves. I certainly must not let them think that I have written something subversive of faith or morals, something blasphemous or irreverent, or even something much more rash and liberal than I have actually written. Nor, on the other hand, must I retain their trust and confidence in myself, and perhaps at the expense of their confidence in those who have condemned me, by allowing them to suppose I have written something perfectly and palpably innocuous, and that there is nothing whatever to be said on the other side.

For though my friends are my chief creditors, I must acknowledge, freely and spontaneously, that a debt is also due to that ecclesiastical authority which as a Catholic I not merely respect and defer to absolutely within its proper limits, but whose rights have been both directly and indirectly the cause to which my life and labours have been devoted.

Seeing that the express purpose of the Confidential Letter was to dissuade my friend from that breach with the Church which would mean an assertion of individualism and a denial of authority and corporate life; seeing that my whole line of argument was to insist that the reasonable and moderate claims of the Church over the individual were not invalidated by any extravagant interpretation of those claims, it would be a grave inconsistency were I, by silence, to suffer even the informal action of authority in my own case to be judged too unfairly, or were I to leave unexplained what might otherwise seem to be on my part a disobedient resistance to its lawful claims.

While thus hesitating and balancing the

reasons for and against publication, I learnt that an Italian journal, "Lo Spettatore," had solved the problem for me by presenting its readers with a complete translation of the Letter. I say nothing of the literary morality of such a procedure; the practical consequence is my chief concern. Plainly, it is best that I should forestall any similar enterprise on the part of an English publisher by publishing myself the text with such explanations and comments as may best mitigate the ill effects of miscellaneous circulation.

These, then, were some of the principal reasons for publishing the Letter in question. On the other hand, it was "confidential" for the reason already given, so that it would be an unpardonable scandal to give as bread to the multitude what was a strong and dangerous remedy prepared to meet a comparatively small number of desperate cases. Moreover, if it would not actually harm and upset less troubled minds, yet it would so much the more seem to them a very inexcusable and unnecessary bit of "liberalizing" on my part. Hence, plainly it could only be published together with some sort of commentary by way of antidote and justification. But here a greater difficulty lay in my path; for the true sense of what was mainly an answer could only be determined by the question which it attempted to solve. The true context of the whole Letter was to be found in the entire array of difficulties, critico-historical and philosophical, with which it dealt indirectly and by way of evasion and diversion, rather than directly point by point. Could I, in conscience, put such an array of problems before the general reader, who would in all likelihood be far more impressed by the direct attack than by the indirect defence?

It seemed best, therefore, to allow my case to be somewhat weakened by its one-sided presentment rather than strengthen it at the price of causing as much or more distress than it was my design to alleviate. I therefore publish the answer without the question except so far as the latter is implied in and shows through the former, or is explicitly quoted here and there in the notes and comments explanatory of the text.

.   .   .   .   .   .

In one point I feel at a great disadvantage with, I will not say my adversaries or my enemies, but with those who differ from me and

think right to oppose me. It is precisely in my
inability to take this cordially hostile attitude in
controversies of great complexity and uncertainty. Experience and reflection confirm me
daily in the conviction that life is less simple
than we learnt from our copy-books and our catechisms, and that our choices—leastways, those of
any moment—are rarely between good and evil,
divisible as it were with a hatchet, but rather
between courses mixed in varying proportions
of both one and the other. The heroes of moral
romance sail serenely through life's darkest
storms, cheered by the certainty of their faultless rectitude and by the hearty applause of a
thoroughly satisfied conscience. But in real
life it seems to me that such serenity, and the
undoubted force and energy which it secures,
are the privilege not so much of the heroic as of
the unreflective. The law of struggle and competition is not confined to the physiological
world, but extends its sway over the social and
moral life of man, where class conflicts with
class, interest with interest, and duty with duty;
where the victory of one combatant means the
defeat and injury of the other. Benevolence to
the spider means cruelty to the fly; and, con-

versely, to rescue the fly is to rob the spider of his well-earned dinner. Looked at closely, our moral life presents us with the same problem at every turn. Mostly we are so content to have chosen the lesser rather than the greater evil, that we qualify such action as simply good; we so rejoice with the rescued fly that we forget to weep with the disappointed spider. Yet since the Divine Will is behind all; since it fights on both sides, giving energy to conqueror and conquered alike, this one-sided sympathy cannot be the divinest and best. Yet were such egotism and one-sidedness lacking to either combatant, were he always sensitively weighing the rights of his adversary's case, what would become of his nerve and sinew and vigour? Were both sides similarly affected, what would become of that wholesome discipline by which Nature selects the best of each kind? Doubtless the disciples of Socrates—not to mention a greater—were much more confident of the absolute injustice of his judges than he was himself. He was only too well aware that good and evil are inextricably tangled, and that there is always a case for the other side; that for his judges as for himself it was a choice of evils; that subjectively both might well be wholly right, but that objectively both were to some extent necessarily wrong. Had Peter thought so nicely as his Master about the case for those who sat in the seat of Moses, he would have been less prompt to draw and brandish his sword; and doubtless the feebleness of the runaway disciples was in large part due to the absence of egotism and one-sided fanaticism on the part of their Master. A Mahomet's whole-hearted condemnation of his adversaries would have inspired a firmer stand. But, after all, there was something to be said, as the event proved, for the official guardians of the Jewish theocracy, though on the whole they were perhaps more wrong than right. It is, then, inevitable that in the dispensation of Nature which favours the strongest fighter they should go under who weigh their adversaries' claims in the same scales as their own—that they should be crucified, poisoned, or otherwise worsted and eliminated. For my own part, I love to read the cudgel controversialists of bygone days, and to hear the resounding thwacks and thuds of those vigorous blows with which they belaboured one another, and which owed their vigour to the absence of all suspicion of a case for the other side. Nor am I at all sure that if charity suffered, truth may not have gained a good deal by this violent advocacy of its several contradictory aspects and extremes; or that if the combatants themselves were blinded by the dust of their scuffle, the cool onlooker may not have learnt more from their very extravagances than from years of quiet and perhaps apathetic solitary reflection. Nor is the race of cudgel controversialists by any means extinct, though its manners have been softened and its tone lowered to suit a more fastidious day. In the clerical and theological world it still owns extensive territories, and there the traveller from a less bracing clime may yet be refreshed by the converse of men who most heartily believe that there is absolutely nothing to be said in favour of their opponents' position. With such men I necessarily feel at a considerable disadvantage, since I must allow them a good deal, whereas they will allow me nothing at all. I must allow that this "Letter to a Professor," though the less of two evils, was nevertheless an evil in some degree, and, while I consider myself justified in having written it, I must allow that those who have condemned me for writing it may also be justified.

I have often wondered whether, if all the circumstances were known, the priest and Levite, whose conduct is contrasted with that of the Good Samaritan, might not have had much to urge in extenuation of their apparent heartlessness. There are duties of non-interference, of minding one's own business; there are the evils of indiscriminate charity; there are the perils of mere impulsiveness to be considered. A large experience of "distress cases" often teaches the priest and Levite a slow caution which seems callousness to the tender-hearted amateur philanthropist. It may be that their charity was not less than the Samaritan's, but that it was more educated; that a prudent casuistry had taught them to balance the claims of conflicting duties; and that before their mental debate was finished they had passed by and left the sufferer behind.

Similarly, he who should hesitate to throw a rope to a drowning man until he had obtained leave of the owner, or who should fear to come promptly to the rescue in any other dubiously lawful way, is not one whom we can condemn absolutely. Yet, on the whole, our sympathy will ever be with the more unscrupulous and impulsive charity that does not reckon the rights and wrongs too nicely, but makes a bold dash for the nearest means to its end.

It is to such an unscrupulous impulse that the "Letter to a Professor" owes its conception and birth; and though no understanding (were such possible) of all the circumstances could clear it from certain taints of original sin and illegitimacy, yet it would do much to spread a fair mantle of charity over these disfiguring blemishes.

The drowning soul now in question was one of those men of scientific and historical rather than of philosophical culture, who are content to take their inherited theology for granted until some accident forces them to consider its coherence with that realm of knowledge in which they themselves are specialists. A faithful and devout Catholic at all times, and one who had suffered some considerable inconvenience in the cause of "Clericalism," it is only in mid life that his responsible office brings him into touch with others, both equals and dependents, who have every right to look to him for a reconciliation between the affirmations of science and criticism and those of traditional theology. With all the confidence of devout faith he throws himself into what he believes will be an easy task, only to find himself more and more entangled in its perplexities. The confessor to whom he first presents his own difficulties demands of him what would be equivalent to a renunciation of his whole education and acquired mentality as the only condition under which he can remain a Catholic. Another confessor takes a wider and vaguer view of the case. A third is as intransigent as the first. And so on. Finally, a prelate too busy to attend to the case himself, yet unwilling to let so large a fish slip the net of Peter, suggests my name with those of two or three others to my friend, who naturally enough turns to the man he knows already rather than to the more competent strangers.

Were it not that my method of dealing with such cases has always been indirect, I might well have refused the responsibility of ministering to the diseases of a mind so much abler and more instructed than my own; but such medicine as I have, and I hope it is no quackery, is a kind of panacea suitable for all sorts of intelligences, high and low; one which cannot do harm, and which within my narrow experience has rarely failed to do good.

It consists in removing the yoke which galls, so as to give the sore place a chance of healing. It assumes that if a man is absolutely and practically sincere to whatever little measure of religious and moral truth he still holds, he is bound to advance to whatever fuller measure of truth may be necessary for him. It assumes that nothing short of conscious and deliberate wickedness of some kind or other can separate a man from communion with Christ and His Church. It declines to admit the existence of any such wickedness in those whose whole trouble is due solely to their anxiety to think, say, and do what is right. It has no sympathy with indifferentism; for it regards a desire to possess the truth as the very test and proof of sincerity; yet while it holds the desire of truth to be essential, it allows that the possession may be often dispensable. In short, it consists in finding out what a man does believe, and building on that; in fostering the sound and healthy parts of his soul instead of physicking the unhealthy—nay, in cutting these off, as far as may be, by diverting from them that nervous attention which can only irritate and spread inflammation through the whole system.

This is the reason of the stress which the Letter lays on the distinction between faith in the Christian revelation, in Christ as a Person, in the Church as a living corporation; and theology which strives to translate revelation from the imaginative language of prophecy into the conceptual language of contemporary scientific thought; which strives to define Christ and to define the Church so as to satisfy the exigencies of our understanding and bring it into harmony with the deeper intuitions of faith. The understanding is subject to a process of rapid transformation from generation to generation. According as the results of experience, observation, and inquiry accumulate, new arrangements, new systems of classification, new methods are requisite to deal with this tangle of matter and get it into serviceable shape and order. It is the function of theology to find place in this system for the truths of the Christian revelation, to translate the unchanging imaginative presentment of prophetic utterance into the shifting terms of current conceptual language. Obviously, to keep pace with the progress of language is necessary under pain of becoming unintelligible, or worse. Yet circumstances for which no one is to blame may for a time isolate one section of the community from the rest and make it lag behind; in which case it will adhere mainly to the older speech or develop it along lines of its own. In such case it is not possible to make up arrears in a moment, and at once to fall into line with the main body again.

It is just those whose mentality is specifically modern, whose minds are well knit together and unified by the categories and methods of current thought, who will necessarily realize the difficulty of assimilating a theology fabricated to suit the mentality of an earlier day, and couched in conceptual language many of whose terms have either become obsolete or, still worse, have so shifted their meaning as to be positively misleading. The ordinary untrained or half-trained mind is too consciously jumbled to be sensitive to or intolerant of that clash of contradictory elements which is so painful to one whose lifelong preoccupation has been the pursuit of unity and coherence. It is easy to counsel patience to those to whom the presence of undigested matter in their mental system causes no pain whatever, but more active minds demand a different treatment. A synthesis they will have, yet to synthesize elements taken from largely heterogeneous mental systems is a feat beyond the capacity of even the ablest individual, and one demanding the slow and difficult co-operation of many minds. Pending the tardy results of such collective labour, I see no relief for minds of the more active and exigent sort but in a clearer and better understanding of the relation between revelation and theology; between faith and theological assent; between religion and the scientific formulation of religion. Of the natural necessity of theology; of a harmony between the concepts of the understanding and the deep intuitions of faith, there can be no doubt; nor should the temporary impossibility of such a concord ever be acquiesced in or accepted as normal and healthy.[1] Yet it is equally evident that, however closely allied and dependent the

[1] See "The Rights and Limits of Theology"; *Quarterly Review*, October, 1905; and more particularly, *Lex Credendi*, pp. 139 ff.

interests of the mind and the heart may be in general, they are not tied together by any law of "convariance" that holds for individual cases. We cannot say that the deepest faith always goes hand-in-hand with the most correct theology, or that they may not often be in precisely inverse proportion one to another. Religious experience, like every other sort of experience, is largely wasted for future and general utility unless it be subjected to the reflection of the understanding. Yet though such understanding enables us to control and command a fuller experience than were otherwise possible, it does not hinder the fact that experience may come to us, and come more abundantly, in other ways. Much as the soil will yield to art in a stubborn clime, it will yield far more to unassisted Nature elsewhere; and similarly, for all the service theology may render to faith, we may find a maximum of faith consistent in certain circumstances with a minimum of theology.

I am convinced that it is a fallacy to appeal to Christ's seeming anti-theological attitude in favour of non-dogmatic religion. His opposition, in this as in other matters, was to the abuse not to the use of the external and institutional side of religion. We are too apt to regard His informal wayside prayings and preachings as the substance of His religion, and not merely as a supplement; to forget that He lived and died a practising Jew; that if He was opposed to legalism, formalism, sacerdotalism, and the other diseases to which religion is liable, He accepted and reverenced the law and the forms, and the priesthood and the sacrifices of the religion of His fathers. Yet it is equally plain that His emphasis was all on the danger of exalting the external over the internal, theology over faith; and on the preference to be given to the latter in case of conflict.

To-day such conflict as there is, is due not to the fact that Christian theology takes account of that Revelation which is its very subject-matter, but to the fact that for centuries it has in many cases treated the prophetic and inspired language of Revelation as possessing exact philosophical or scientific value, and has thus deduced prosaic conclusions from quasi-poetical premisses; proving, e.g., the non-existence of the Antipodes from: "Every eye shall behold Him"; or the immobility of the earth from:

"He hath established the round world so that it shall never be moved." In the measure that hundreds of such premisses, immutable because revealed, have been woven into its texture and made to support whole chains of deduction, dogmatic theology has grown more and more out of joint with the rest of science. The other sciences have arrived too late (if they have yet quite arrived) at a clear consciousness of their own proper scope and method to afford to throw stones; especially since from the nature of the case the relation of theology to its subject-matter is exceedingly complex. For it deals, not with the divine realities and facts themselves, but with that imaginative prophetic presentment of them which is, as it were, their moving, living shadow—something as real and concrete as themselves; by no means conceptual or intellectual, as theology has sometimes forgotten.

I do not, then, think that a temporary embarrassment of theology is something very surprising or very alarming; least of all in the case of any particular individual whose faith and good will are abundantly evident, and who therefore has got the "root of the matter" in him.

.   .   .   .

So much being premised, I now propose to go through the following letter in company with the patient reader, and point out on the road anything that may deserve explanation or comment.

A LETTER

TO A UNIVERSITY PROFESSOR

Dear ——,

I thought it better to leave your letter unanswered all these weeks than answer it hastily or less fully than I now propose to do. As a teacher and professor you will understand how much easier it is to be brief in propounding problems than in solving them, and will therefore pardon an unavoidable prolixity which wearies me in one way, if it wearies you in another.

No, I am neither surprised, nor shocked nor alarmed at your candid confession, but only sincerely sorry for your temporary distress of mind, and earnestly anxious to do all I can to alleviate that distress, even though I should be unable to remove it altogether.

I am "not surprised," because in point of fact the percentage of educated Catholics who are similarly troubled is necessarily and rapidly on the increase: and because unfortunately so many of them refer, or are referred, to me in their perplexities (as though I were the inventor of some secret panacea) that I get a somewhat exaggerated impression of their numerical proportion to the untroubled many, and begin to regard them as representing the rule rather than its exceptions. To many a priest even of wide experience and repute the very existence of such a class is unknown save by remote hearsay—thus by a sort of magnetism do we each select and fashion a little world of our own which we too readily mistake for the universe, for the sole possible world. I am therefore only too well used to such revelations; and moreover all that I know of your antecedents and circumstances, of the trend of your thoughts and your private studies, of the set into which your profession has thrown you, and of your special intimacies and interests, has prepared me for this almost inevitable *dénouement*.

As I am "not surprised" so neither am I "shocked" as though my estimate of your moral worth had suddenly been proved false or exaggerated. The inclination to ascribe the denial

on the part of others of our own beliefs and
opinions to stupidity, immorality and bad faith
is as unchristian as it is uncritical. Only when
we take the word "Faith" in its ethical and
evangelical sense, is it true to say that loss of
faith necessarily implies some moral weakness
or imperfection. To this I shall have more to
add presently. But the saying is palpably false
when faith is made to stand for theological
orthodoxy, for assent to a dogmatic system. It
is admitted on all hands that such faith as this
may, and often does, go with the extremest
moral depravity—with sensuality and cruelty
and injustice and untruthfulness and hypocrisy.
Prejudice and superstition; temporal and selfish
interests of one sort or another; or more commonly still an absolute lack of all sympathetic
and intelligent interest in their religion will keep
the great majority of such men in the paths of
orthodoxy as long as orthodoxy is in public
fashion and favour. Of this sort, nowise interested in the truth of religion for its own sake,
the presumption holds good that their revolt
against orthodoxy may always be explained by
some less worthy motive. That they themselves
should hold this explanation to be in all cases

the only possible and conceivable one, is of course very understandable; but that there is another, is also perfectly obvious. Indeed theologians themselves allow for the case of blameless or "invincible" ignorance—of mental incapacity. Convinced as they were of the perfectly self-evident character of their principles and facts, and of the mathematical cogency of their deductions therefrom; crediting the intellectual system itself with that firmness which only belonged to their own hold on it in a Catholic age and country where no other system was subjectively thinkable, they formerly limited the excuse of "invincible ignorance" (as far as Christians were concerned) to cases of quite abnormal mental incapacity. But times have changed, and what with the relative inertness and immutability of orthodox theology on the one side, and the inconceivably rapid expansion of knowledge and of means and methods of inquiry on the other, difficulties have accumulated to a degree that makes the ablest and most cultivated minds to be those least capable of effecting a reconciliation between orthodox theology and the rest of the field of knowledge. For one reason or another theologians have, for generations, been letting their accounts get into disorder; they have trusted to the one general principle of "authority" for the quieting of all possible doubts and have paid less and less attention to particulars. They have forgotten that, by a necessary law of the mind, the claims of authority will *de facto* inevitably be called in question as soon as the reasons on which those claims rest are cancelled or outweighed by those which stand against the particular teachings of authority; that though a Catholic as such cannot consistently call this or that Catholic doctrine in question, he can[1] consistently call his Catholicism in question. The most trusted and competent teacher may presume on his credit and make assertions so extravagant as to force us at last to doubt his veracity or his sanity. To believe him might involve a denial of the very principles and sentiments on which our trust in him originally depended.

I can easily imagine that for many a one the "cumulative" argument against Catholicism might be relatively and subjectively far stronger than that in its favour; and that for such a one assent had, without any shadow of fault on his

[1] As far as logic goes.

side, become a mental impossibility. On the contrary, had he been more worldly-minded, less interested in religion for his own sake and for the sake of others, he might have preserved his orthodoxy undisturbed.

But by some it might be counted to you as a fault that you allowed yourself to be overwhelmed by these difficulties; that you exaggerated your own mental strength, whereas it was your duty to protect your faith by shutting your eyes or by running away from dangers.

Now, however unwilling a man may be to raise doubts in his own mind, he cannot live in an age and country like yours without their being thrust upon his attention at every turn. In mediæval Spain, where index and inquisition were practically workable methods of protection, it was otherwise. There and then one only needed not to *think* in order to be at peace; here and now one needs also not to see or hear or read or converse or live. There is now no educational grade so low as to be exempt entirely from the spirit of criticism, whose influence is of course still more strongly felt as we ascend to the higher grades. Where faith was a matter of course with all, one was never challenged for a reason for one's convictions;

but where dissensions and negations are the rule, the challenge is perpetual and must compel one to reflect on, and criticize one's position.

And then, behind this warning against over-rating one's wisdom by measuring swords with one's intellectual betters, lies the supposition that we are encroaching on the rights of a privileged class; that if for the majority such an endeavour be presumptuous, there is a minority for whom it is a duty, and who are competent to acquit themselves of that duty. It is implied that modesty bids us trust to these experts and distrust ourselves. But apart from the obvious objection that there are experts on the opposite sides in every great controversy; that doctors differ and that the layman and the unlearned must at last choose between them either on caprice, or by some exercise of private judgment and criticism—apart from this, we may ask: Who are these experts who can and ought to face these difficulties, and who have faced them? Certainly if we turn to the clergy we find a great readiness on the part of individuals to disclaim the honour, and also a curious vagueness as to its precise depositaries.[1] Taken individually,* they frankly say that they are themselves incom-

* For Notes see end of Letter.

petent to deal with such problems, but they imply that they have an unbounded confidence in their own collectivity, or in certain persons, unknown and unknowable, whose speciality it is to adjust the claims of sacred and secular knowledge. Thus the responsibility divided over the whole multitude of the Church's children is shifted from shoulder to shoulder, and comes to rest nowhere in particular; nor is there, we are prone to suspect, any solid cash answering to these paper-notes that pass from hand to hand. Surely, if there is any class of Catholics either fit, or bound to make itself fit to deal with these matters, it is the class to which you belong by profession, the class of savants and university professors whose duty it is to dispense the fruits of culture to the young men of the rising generation.[2] It is to the class from which the ablest criticism of religion derives that we should look for the ablest counter-criticism and defence of religion. If you and your peers must shut your eyes to difficulties, then who on earth is free to face them? Is there no faith anywhere in the world that can bear the full light of day? Is voluntary or involuntary ignorance its universal and necessary condition? And then the very nature of your studies, historical, philological and philosophical, in every way bearing critically on religion; and the keen controversies of your non-Catholic friends and colleagues about Christian origins and developments; and your position in relation to the Catholic undergraduates who looked to you far more than to their clergy for an understanding sympathy with their dawning perplexities—these and countless other reasons not only justified your criticism of Catholicism, but made it a plain duty.

So far then from being "shocked" at what to some might seem to imply a falling away from higher standards and principles, I can well imagine that your present unfortunate predicament is actually the result of your conscientious fidelity to those principles.

As I am not "surprised" nor "shocked," so neither am I "alarmed" by your self-revelation; certainly far less alarmed than you yourself seem to be. I do not underrate the moral and spiritual dangers of one who finds all his old landmarks suddenly obliterated; all his guides discredited; all his authorities called in doubt; of one who finds himself no longer supported and carried

along in the crowd of which he had been a part
and by whose customs and ways of thought,
speech, and action he had been determined far
more than he ever suspected till the support
gave way; of one who is thrown upon himself,
as it were dropped down in the midst of a path-
less desert, to find his own way and fend for
himself as best he can. I can imagine a man
brought to such a pass by no fault of his own;
nay, in consequence of his strict inward truth-
fulness and fidelity, and yet losing his head
when he views himself, not in the mirror of his
own conscience, but as we are so prone to do,
in the mirror of popular opinion; I can fancy
his independence of judgment which has carried
him so far, breaking down wearily just at this
critical point, refusing to justify him in his own
eyes, and persuading him that he has thrown in
his lot with the irreligious and taken a lower
moral platform. It is hard suddenly to resist
the verdict of the little *orbis terrarum* to which
he has deferred from childhood and not to *feel*
wrong even when he *knows* he is right. And
then there is that other *orbis terrarum*, formerly
hostile, now ready to welcome him as a convert
and recruit, ignorant of the unwillingness, the

reluctance, the hesitancy of his accession to
their ranks; dense to the differences which he
conceives still to separate his position infinitely
from theirs, as light from darkness. It is not
easy to stand solitary and aloof between the two
camps, drawn to the one by kindnesses and
flatteries, driven from the other by vituperations and slanders. What wonder if he begin
to rate himself as others rate him, and end by
being what he thus falsely believes himself to
be! That is a danger to which the best of men
might be exposed, yet it is not one to which it
is necessary or likely that you will fall a victim,
and therefore I am not alarmed. I see no
reason to fear that you will ever be less sincere
and conscientious and essentially religious-
minded than you always have been and are
now. You may perhaps never see your way
any more clearly than at present, yet "God is
with us in the night, who made the darkness
and the light, and dwells not in the light alone,
but in the darkness and the cloud."

I have read very carefully the MS. which
accompanied your letter and which contains the
sum and substance of your indictment against,
I will not say, Catholicism, but rather against

the theological presentment and defence of Catholicism. I can honestly say, it contained nothing that was new to me; no difficulty to whose force I am insensible. Indeed in many a case I could have dotted the *i* and crossed the *t*. I am quite alive to the far-reaching consequences of Scripture-criticism especially as applied to the Gospels, and to its direct and indirect bearing on the Church's claims to infallibility. I see that there are not really, as might seem on the surface, two Catholic parties who, having both fairly faced the evidences of the critics, have reached opposite conclusions (conservative and radical) as to their significance; but that moral unanimity prevails among them just in the measure that they have appropriated the evidence; that the conservative positions are maintained by ignorance, systematic or involuntary. I see how the close historical study of Christian origins and developments must undermine many of our most fundamental assumptions in regard to dogmas and institutions. I see how the sphere of the miraculous is daily limited by the growing difficulty in verifying such facts, and the growing facility of reducing either them or the belief in them to natural and recognized causes. I see and feel moreover how these and like objections would be as nothing could we point triumphantly to the Christian ethos of the Church, to the religious spirit developed by her system as by no other; and were there not in the approved writings of her ascetical teachers, and her moralists; in the prevailing practices of her confessors and directors; in the liturgical biographies of her canonized saints; in the principles of her government and in her methods of education, much that revolts the very same moral and religious sense to which in the first instance her claims to our submission must appeal. Here indeed, as you say, we are involved seemingly in self-contradiction; as soon, namely, as authority bids us repudiate the very principles and sentiments on which alone our obedience to it can rest.[3]

I might perhaps (though to little purpose) deal with these difficulties in detail; but I agree with you that if, as Newman says, the cumulative argument, the verdict of the inferential sense, is to be admitted in favour of the Church's claim, it must also be admitted on the other side; and therefore that a man may, by the insensible accumulation and confluence of small difficulties, each no more than a probability, find the balance turned some fine day without being able to credit the result to any particular hair in the scale. His negation may be subjectively justified (at least intellectually) without his being able or bound to offer any distinct dialectical proof thereof. In your case, I see that it is so; and even were I able—which I am not—to deal satisfactorily with the formulated expression of your difficulties, I can quite imagine that your general impression would remain unchanged, that you would only feel you had made a false diagnosis of your ailment.

As to the reasons you have put down on paper, I might quarrel with some of them in detail; but taken all together they constitute a massive objection against received theological positions which, frankly, I am unable to solve. Nor will I pretend that in this I am modestly deferring to the more competent, for I am quite unable to satisfy your alternative request and refer you to some better-informed theologian as a substitute for myself. I could send you to A who is alive to one side of the problem, or to B, C, and D who are alive to others; but to no one who at once sees all round it and professes to have reached a constructive solution. All would at a given point make confession of their ignorance and of their faith in the faith of others. The plain truth is that nobody in the Church yet knows the solution which, if it exists at all, exists piecemeal among many minds, or lies potentially in the depths of the collective subconsciousness of the faithful at large.

Let it be granted, for argument's sake, that things are quite as bad as you say, and that the intellectual defence of Catholicism breaks down on every side as far as you are concerned; or that at least your mental confusion is so hopeless that you dare not commit yourself to any affirmation one way or the other — does it straightway follow you should separate yourself from the communion of the Church? Yes, if theological "intellectualism" be right; if faith mean mental assent to a system of conceptions of the understanding; if Catholicism be primarily a theology or at most a system of practical observances regulated by that theology. No, if Catholicism be primarily a life, and the Church a spiritual organism in whose life we participate, and if theology be but an attempt of that life to formulate and understand itself— an attempt which may fail wholly or in part without affecting the value and reality of the said life.[4]

We are familiar now with the distinction between the conscious and the subconscious in the individual; still more between a man's diagnosis of himself and what he really is, unknown to himself; between the sum-total of memories and ideas, of deliberate aims, purposes, and intentions of which he is, or can freely make himself, conscious; and that immeasurably vaster resultant of forgotten and unregistered experiences personal or ancestral, and of impulses and tendencies determined by the same experiences, which constitute his unknown, unformulated self, compared with which his freely-fashioned, conscious, formulated self is as but the emergent point of a submerged mountain whose roots broaden out till they are merged with the bulk of the entire earth.

Our active life as free, self-forming personalities, is necessarily limited by the character and capacities of this buried soul which is committed to our cultivation, as it were, an unknown wilderness. In the measure that we come to understand more truly the nature of the soil and climate we shall reap more abundant returns and shall be able to render the soil itself more fruitful. True, the husbandman works for the sake of the fruit, and not for the sake of work; whereas our active and spiritual (as opposed to our passive and psychic) life is an end in itself, and the psychic produce is but subordinate and secondary. It is the struggle, the thought, the labour, the conflict with the stubborn soil, with the weeds and briers, with the caprices of climate, that constitute our truest personality; what we make ourselves actively, not what we find ourselves passively; what we would be, not what we are. But how often do we diagnose ourselves partly or wholly amiss! How little do we understand of our deepest beliefs and feelings; of our strengths and weaknesses; of our capacities and incapacities for good or for evil! How often are we surprised and thrown out in our calculations by "up-rushes," as they are called, of passions or convictions or irresistible determinations—by "possessions" as it were of alien spirits counter to our conscious voluntary self—and forced perhaps to reconstruct our whole theory of ourselves from the foundations, to readjust the whole system of our aims and purposes— like a physician suddenly aware that he has radically misjudged the case before him!

Well, if this be hardly questionable as psychology of the individual, it is far more evident by way of analogy when we deal with states and societies and communities. There, obviously, a good representative government is supposed to gauge and formulate the mind and will and sentiments of the governed masses, and to bring them to consciousness. So far as it does so correctly, it is instrumental in the civilizing and improvement of those masses; in bringing them into spontaneous sympathy with the laws of their growth and development. But how seldom is this realized! and how often is revolution the only possible remedy of bad government based on total miscalculation of the disruptive forces—the ideas, sentiments, and tendencies—buried in the collective subconsciousness!

Can we be very far wrong in applying all this to the Christian Society, to the Catholic Church?[5] Must we not there too distinguish

between the collective subconsciousness of the
"People of God" and the consciously formulated mind and will of the governing section of
the Church? May not our faith in the latter be
at times weak or nil, and yet our faith in the
former strong and invincible?[6]

We know that the psychic subconscious self
of the individual is a very wilderness of conflicting elements, good and evil, false and true;
and that it is the task and very life of the free,
conscious spiritual self to develop the better, to
repress the worse; and that the resultant owes
its individuality not wholly to the freedom of
our choice, but also to the limits and character of
its subject-matter (i.e. of the psychic, passive,
subconscious self). It is idle to deny that some
have a happier temperament, a less thorny and
stubborn soil to deal with, than others; that
their spontaneous uncultivated judgments and
tendencies are more generally on the side of
reason and right. If it is true that, in some
degree, the free spiritual self succeeds in
modifying and improving the psychic self, in
training it, so to say, to a more willing and
effectual serviceableness; it is also true that
the psychic self, in its own order, by its passive

resistances or its propensions, can obstruct or further the development of the free self, can present to it temptations or "graces," vicious or virtuous inclinations. There is a practical limit to what a man can make out of himself; there are good or evil propensities which he may overcome for a time, but which will assert themselves again and again as long as he lives. Hence we feel sure of some men that though they may go wrong for a time they will come right again; and of others, that though they keep right for a time yet they will fall again sooner or later. In the one case we have faith in the man; in the other we have not. Analogously, it seems to me that a man might have great faith in the Church, in the people of God, in the unformulated ideas, sentiments and tendencies at work in the great body of the faithful, and constituting the Christian and Catholic "Spirit"; and yet regard the Church's consciously formulated ideas and intentions about herself as more or less untrue to her deepest nature; that he might refuse to believe her own account of herself as against his instinctive conviction of her true character; that he might say to her: *Nescitis cujus spiritus estis*—"You know not your own essential spirit." (Cf. Note 6.)

Hence it seems to me that unless a man identifies Catholicism with the formulated ideas and intentions of those in whom at the present moment the spirit of the whole body of the faithful strives to arrive at some degree of self-consciousness or self-understanding, his quarrel with the expression is no reason *per se* for quarrelling with the thing expressed—any more than his dissatisfaction with the political theory and action of his country's representatives would be a reason for denying his nationality. "But who," you will ask, "is to say what Catholicism is if not the official representatives of this Society? if not her Popes, Councils, Bishops, theologians?" No one, *officially or with authority;* but when authority is dumb or stultifies itself, private conviction resumes its previous rights and liberties. It sent us to authority in the first instance not by a suicidal self-contradictory act; but in basing our trust upon reasons and sentiments it thereby assigned a limit to that trust which is reached as soon as authority would seem to violate those reasons or sentiments.

Again, it is not absolutely necessary that anybody should be able to say precisely and adequately what Catholicism is. We can live and be, without knowing how to explain and define ourselves; the greater and healthier part of mankind do so.

The truth is, that our official representatives and exponents, those in whose mind Catholicism tries to define itself, being but mortals, are dominated by a sort of corporate or class interest, and are prone to exaggerate their own importance and to identify themselves with "the Church" much as social and political theorists and agitators are prone to identify themselves with the people, with the great silent masses of the population too busied about living to think how or why they live. We are apt to be passively receptive under the self-assertion and self-advertisement of a class whose interest it is to prove its own services to the community to be as indispensable as possible, to show that there is no hope for us unless we accept their views, follow their directions, and buy their wares. Though the inert multitude cannot or will not controvert these claims, it does not take them quite seriously, but opposes a considerable common-sense passive resistance to them.

A MUCH-ABUSED LETTER 59

We do not buy our grocer's tea because he says it is the cheapest and best in the world, but because we have tried it and found it satisfy our more moderate requirements. Let us then clear our mind of illusion and recognize that, in spite of its noisy advertisements, this self-conscious, self-formulating Catholicism of the thinking, talking, and governing minority is not the whole Church, but only an element (however important) in its constitution.[7]

Is it not because you forget this that the prospect seems to you so hopeless? Is it not because you are looking forward to the necessary developments of the ideas and principles of formulated and organized Catholicism and taking no account of the inscrutable voiceless life which it strives feebly to formulate, of the eternal truths, the Divine instincts that work themselves out irresistibly in the heart of the whole people of God? Every "Active" is limited by the receptivity of its "Passive"; as the artist is by the capacity of his tools and his materials. To forecast the future developments of Catholicism we must look to those of lay receptivity as well as to those of theological or legislative activity; and as they are on the whole in contrary directions it may be hoped they will healthily neutralize each other's defects and excesses.

I do not then see why, from your own present point of view, your inability to understand and sympathize with theoretical Catholicism should necessarily separate you from the body of the faithful—so long as you are not required in any way to belie your inmost sentiments and beliefs. But of course I am supposing the existence of certain positive reasons, of heart, if not of head, which bind you to the Church, that is, to the body of those who are united throughout the world and across the centuries under the denomination of Catholic and Roman; I am supposing that though formulated Catholicism does violence to your intelligence and your moral sense, yet unformulated Catholicism, or rather the living multitudinous reality thus perversely formulated, draws and holds you to itself by ties of affection and of instinctive spiritual sympathy. I am only showing that the breakdown of the formula does not at once alter the nature, or peril the existence, of the reality, nor of your relations to it. You are, I perceive, as clear as ever against the psychological fallacies of individualism in religion; you see that, like the musical or any other artistic or spiritual capacity, that of religion needs the educational influence of a widespread and permanent Society for its development and progress ; that it needs its schools, its teachers, its great masters, its laymen and its experts, its traditions and rules and principles and criteria. Moreover, in the measure that it takes the form of a universal and world-wide Society, a religion needs an organization whereby its parts may be brought to bear upon one another, and its ideas, desires, and energies, scattered among millions, may be focussed to a point, and determined to a common resultant.

You see also that the principle of schism or disintegration is *per se* a very mischievous one ; that it contracts the area of that collective life and experience which it is the function of such a society to gather up from all, and to digest and distribute in the form of nutriment to each; that the schismatic body or individual is cut off the living organism and from its historical past ; that schism deprives the organism of the force of certain vigorous ideas and impulses which, working within the restrictions of its periphery, would have eventually modified its permanent character throughout, and perhaps saved the said ideas and impulses from the fate, as it were, of steam that has escaped from the boiler, the pressure of whose prisoning walls was the secret of its utility. Here, at least, we are cordially at one—namely, in holding that from the nature of things schism is hurtful, Catholicism conducive, to the richest development and diffusion of Christianity.

We both see in the Catholic and Roman Church the unbroken extension of the little society gathered round Jesus of Galilee two thousand years ago; we both condemn every voluntary schism as a mistake, not on the Philistine ground that the Church was all right [8] and the Schismatics all wrong; but, contrariwise, because there were vigorous vital elements of goodness and truth in nearly every schism, which were thus dissipated and lost to the Church.

Again, I think you agree with me, that though the one thing needful is communion with the invisible Church (i.e. with God as presented to us in Christ and in all Christ-like men past, present and future; with all those who, whatever their professed creed, in any way or degree suffer and forsake themselves for God's cause and God's will), yet communion with the visible Church, with those, namely, who *profess* to be Christ-like, is a great *desideratum*, is a condition of more fruitful communion with the invisible. For, besides the more obvious reasons which will occur to every one, there is a depth, height, width, and fulness added to our inward life by our conscious and sympathetic association with a great world-wide cause or work such as that of Catholicism; something analogous to the spiritual expansion produced in us by an intelligent, self-sacrificing and active participation in the life of our state or country. If God's cause on earth should be championed by each individual, it is certainly rational that, like other causes, it should be championed by a society; not merely by knights errant, but by an organized army. In the Catholic Church, God's cause on earth, the cause of Christianity, of Religion in its highest development, finds its visible embodiment and instrument.

The Church is, after all, the development of what was primarily an apostolic, propagandist, or missionary body sent forth to preach and prepare the Kingdom of God, and is itself a "Kingdom of God" only in a secondary sense. What personal religion should be among the factors of our inward personal life (principal but distinct; as the head is the principal part of the organism distinct from the others), that the Catholic Church should be among the other factors or instruments of our public civilization. Plainly, I do not mean a sectarian Catholicism at war with heretics; nor a political Catholicism at war with the States; but simply a spiritual society organized purely in the interests of religion and morality. To belong to this world-wide, authentic, and original Christian society, to appropriate its universal life as far as possible, to be fired with its best enthusiasms, to devote oneself to its services and aims, is to go out of one's selfish littleness and to enter into the vast collective life—the hopes and fears, joys and sorrows, failures and successes—of all those millions who have ever borne, or bear, or shall yet bear the name of Catholic, and who have in any degree lived worthy of that name.

Reasons like these may hold a man fast to the Church by a thousand ties of affection and loyalty, of moral, religious, and Christian sentiment, which can in no way be weakened by any collapse of his intellectual formulation of Catholicism.

"But," you will object—and this brings me to the main purpose of my letter—"this collapse of the intellectual position, this confusion and at least temporary agnosticism as to the true value of dogmas and sacraments, as to nearly all that theologians impose upon us under pain of anathema, does not stop with the brain, but strikes paralysis into all the members. Action may be in one sense prior to belief, and more important; but it is not wholly independent of it; there is a mutual exchange of services, an organic unity which excludes absolute priority. Can I go on living with the Church's life when I can no longer see with her eyes or think with her mind? You say, 'Live the religion, test it experimentally, and you will come to see and feel its truth.' Yes, but to believe in it is an essential part of the very life in question, and one on which many of the other parts are dependent."

Here again I think you should be slow to take theology as seriously as theologians would have us take it; you should discount for their class-interest and for the necessary one-sidedness of all specialism. After all, the Catholic outlook is larger than the clerical. Naturally the theologian is tempted to bring his whole system in all its details and connexions under the ægis of Faith, and by ignoring the difference between the facts of religious experience and their analysis and expression, to make out that no man can live the life of faith unless he have first accepted the whole theological analysis of that life. This of course is at variance with reason and experience and with the whole character of that Gospel which was preached to the simple and hidden from the sophists. If in the Athanasian Creed the words "This is the Catholic Faith which except a man believe faithfully he cannot be saved" referred, as they seem, to the foregoing theological analysis, they would be ridiculous. Their only tolerable sense is: "This is the analysis of the Catholic Faith, of those facts and truths by which a man must live (or, of that supernatural world in which he must live) if he is to be saved."

If you will put aside these class-estimates of the matter, and look into your own spiritual experience, I think you will see that the truths by which you really live and grow are few and simple, and too fundamental to be involved in the fate of anything so contingent as a theological system; that even what is most characteristically Christian and Catholic in the lives of the greatest saints has but little dependence on the complexities of ecclesiastical teachings and ordinances, and as a fact obtained among the apostles and first disciples of Christ, generations before the said complexities were called into existence.

And certainly faith is the very root and all-permeating inspiration of that life. Not the faith of mere obedience to authoritative teaching, which is at best a condition of spiritual education, a means of wakening dormant faculties, of providing healthy food to be digested and vitally assimilated by the recipient; not the faith of merely intellectual assent to the historical and metaphysical assertions of a theology that claims to be miraculously guaranteed from errancy.

Where do we find Christ insisting on the spiritual necessity or advantage of beliefs that perplex or do violence to the senses and intelligence of His hearers, except so far as He rebukes their lack of that deeper intelligence which is conditioned by moral dispositions and is kin to, if not identical with Faith? For Faith is "the substance of things hoped for, the evidence of things not seen." It is a realizing, a making substantial to ourselves, of that world of hopes as yet so far removed from our grasp and clear vision as to be no more than a poet's or prophet's dream. It is to live as though that unseen world were already self-evident to us, to reckon with it as with part of our environment. Whether we will or no, we are constrained in every free and deliberate action of our lives to assume some theory of life and its value, be it even that of the pure agnostic; we are forced to an implicit affirmation of what is unprovable; we cannot act *in vacuo*, or move in no direction at all. Proximate ends indeed fall within the range of our senses and reason, but the ultimate ends with which they are continuous lie in the darkness beyond; so that faith of some sort—Divine, worldly or agnostic—must be the ultimate guide and directive of all our actions. We know that the world does not explain itself, that the explanation must lie in that "beyond" or "behind" into which faith peers, in that Whole of which sense and reason give us but some infinitesimal fraction. But though our belief as to the character of that whole, our belief in the "Yea" of Religion or in the "Nay" of Omar Khayyam or of Ecclesiastes, be a matter of a free choice by which we stand or fall, self-judged; yet it is not an arbitrary or capricious choice, but one based on a power of vision that is conditioned by our self-formed character, by our moral dispositions. Faith is a *seeing* of God, not face to face but through a glass darkly; still it is a seeing for oneself; not a believing on hearsay.[9] It is a corrective of reasoning, even as reasoning is of immediate sensation; it is an analogous extension of the range of our knowledge and action, as it were, by new methods; it carries us beyond space to immensity; beyond time to eternity; beyond the relative to the absolute. It is a rudimentary faculty relating us to a world which is as yet "future" and "beyond" in respect to our clear consciousness. And we rightly speak of it as "Divine" or Supernatural faith; for this vision is not at command but is given us; and that, most clearly in moments when we seem most filled with God; when we are truest to all that is best in our spiritual nature; when we are lifted up above the plane of ordinary vision, not by some narrowing excitement or intoxicant that excludes the data of sober sense and so produces an illusory transformation of reality; but by an access of inward light which shows us all we knew before, included in a vaster and deeper knowledge, transcended but not contradicted. In such moments we seem to gaze with God's eyes and from the standpoint of the whole. It is as though by certain moral self-adjustments and self-dispositions the soul had first to set its face and strain its eyes in the right direction; and that then God could lift it up to command a wider horizon.

To live by the memory of such moments in the teeth of the doubts and negations of our lower and narrower states is to live the life of Faith; it is, not to ignore fanatically the meanings and values of that world given us by our senses and understanding, but to accommodate our action to the totality of which this is but part and by which it is to be explained. It is to take our stand on the side of such men as those set before us in Hebrews XI. and XII. as types and examples of Faith; men who were as strangers and pilgrims among the men of no faith, among those who could find a home and abiding city upon this earth of shadows and illusions; it is to be on the side of those who "looked for a city that hath foundations, whose builder and maker is God"; of those to whom the invisible ideal future was as effectually real as the visible present and actual; of those in whom the Divine judgment of their spiritual intuitions stood firm and unshaken against the assaults of their narrower reason, against the protest of their lower nature, against the tradition, the influence, the consensus of the multitudes who live or seem to live for the apparent and unreal.

And the object of this faith, the reality thus apprehended, what is it but what Matthew Arnold calls the "Power that makes for Righteousness"? No mere personification of the Ideal, of the abstract conception of all conceivable goodness human and other, but that Force which we feel within ourselves impelling us upward and onward towards the Ideal, towards the Better and Best; a force which we may obey or resist, but in obedience to which alone we can find rest and peace. To think of it as less than personal, as otherwise than spiritual, is not practically possible; nay, we must think of it as absolute, as inexhaustible, as never to be equalled or expressed by any extension or cumulation of that finite goodness whose latent potentialities, yet to be realized, are what we mean by the Ideal. And it is the same force whose workings we recognize in the goodness of our fellow-men of all ages and races and varieties, whom it binds together into one mystical body and brotherhood and shapes to a collective presentment and revelation of itself, and to a society for the furtherance of its own ends. We do not worship Humanity, with the Comtists, but we worship the Power that is revealed in human goodness of every sort. In this sense Humanity, so far as it stands for the just, the noble, the brave and the true, for those who in any way have crucified, sacrificed, limited themselves for the love of God and for the sake of His Kingdom and of their fellow-men, is a mystical Christ, a collective Logos, a Word or Manifestation of the Father; and every member of that society is in his measure a Christ or revealer in whom God is made flesh and dwells in our midst.

If Divine Faith in some degree breaks down the limitations of our finite mind and vision, and makes us sharers in God's vision; if by it we lose our petty separateness and particularity of view and are identified with the Infinite of thought and knowledge through voluntary subjection of the natural to the Divine light that is within us, this apprehension of another world is correlative to another mode of life and love. It is in the light of faith that we live the life of charity, and pass from under the government of self-centred love to that of a love whose centre is everywhere and its circumference nowhere, to that of the love of absolute goodness as revealed in human goodness, of God as revealed in man, of man as (actually or potentially; singly or collectively) revealing God; it is the Whole which now begins to live in us, whose ends and aims and desires we appropriate at the sacrifice of our private and separate ends.

But this divine and supernatural life with its disinterested ideals and enthusiasms is altogether beyond the resources of our natural and separate powers of endurance and abnegation, and beyond our limited psychic and mental energies. Of ourselves we cannot even think, much less desire and perform effectually what is disinterestedly good in the divine and universal sense. Such thoughts and desires and performances do obtain in us all, but only because we are all by our whole nature and destiny instruments of God's working, which mingles with ours in every instant of our inward life. If it is only through Him that we can think and do anything that is really good and divine, it is only through Him that we can do more; it is only by so adjusting ourselves as instruments to His hands that from Him the strength and vigour of the Whole may flow into us and make us equal to the labour and suffering entailed by the service of universal ends—to the strain of a divine life energizing in the frail mechanism of our finite nature.

Thus understood, faith and love and hope are three factors into which the life of religion, of union with God through humanity, with humanity through God, may be resolved. This is a religion which is logically (not historically) older than all the creeds that have struggled so variously to give it expression; just as every kind of life is older than its intellectual analysis. So far as you live with this life you are in spiritual communion, not only with Catholic Christians, but with the men of faith of every creed or no creed through the length and breadth of the world.

But I venture to think that allowing criticism to have been still more successful in its assaults on Catholic positions than even you would be disposed to concede, yet there is and will always be enough left standing to justify you in regarding Catholicism as at once the highest expression or determination and the most effectual instrument of the life of religion, and therefore in abiding peacefully in that communion and living its life so far as others allow you your due liberty and do not seek to bind you to their party-placets.

Society and social organization is the normal condition of our religious, as it is of our moral and rational life and development. Through its mediation we are brought into more fruitful communication with our total environment, with that Whole to which we belong, from which we receive all, to which we must return all—life consisting in that very exchange and commerce. Society makes us heirs of its own collective experience in the past; and starts us in life not as beggars but as capitalists. The truly disinterested social life of a man who lives (not merely in and on his people, but) for his people, in whom the true civic or national spirit dominates over all purely personal and separate interests, may, analogously to the life of religion, be resolved into a sort of faith, charity and hope. For in such a man the general mind and outlook supplants the personal and private; the general ends, interests and affections absorb and transcend the particular; and as an active member of the social organism his internal and external energies are reinforced by those of the whole community which acts with him and through him. In the measure that he enters into the common life it enters into him; the more he gives the more he receives; he becomes wise with its wisdom, strong with its strength, rich with its riches.

But the life of religion, of communion with the Power that makes for Righteousness in man; with God as revealed in men singly and collectively; with men as revealing God—this life obviously needs for its perfect development a society in which all men should be united. There is in fact none such; but this is what

Catholicism is, at least in tendency and aspiration: "Go, make disciples of *all nations,* baptizing them." The Roman communion may be no more than the charred stump of a tree torn to pieces by gales and rent by thunderbolts; she may be and probably is more responsible for all the schisms than the schismatics themselves,[1] yet, unlike them all, she stands for the principle of Catholicity, for the ideal of a spiritually united humanity centred round Christ in one divine society—of the Kingdom of God governed by the Son of God; she is at least an abortive essay towards that perfect all-embracing religious association which as a mediating instrument should secure the fullest and freest commerce between its several members and the Whole; that is, between the soul and God. And when we consider how the seed of the Gospel has drawn into itself all that was richest in the religious soil of Judea (itself nourished by the experiences of older religions of the forgotten past), as well as of Rome and of Greece, and through them of the Eastern world whose wisdom they had plundered; and when we also remember how these materials have been

[1] Cf. Note 8.

wrought upon and informed by the collective spiritual labour of the Church for two thousand years, we must at least acknowledge that her creed embodies the results of the religious experiences of a vast section and period of humanity, that it gives a presentment of the Absolute—of that "Beyond" which faith apprehends and of man's relations to that world—which has a certain practical or regulative truth, and admits, so far, of experimental proof. We must not take it as one might take a sentence and determine its meaning by the etymology of each word singly, neglecting the difference that both use and connexion make in their significance; but rather view it in its entirety as a symbol of that impression of itself which the Infinite has left upon the consciousness of so large and notable a part of mankind. The Trinity, the Creation, the Fall, the Incarnation, the Atonement, the Resurrection, Heaven and Hell, Angels and Devils, the Madonna and the Saints, all are pieces of one mosaic, all, closer determinations of one and the same presentment of the Eternal Goodness in the light of which man must shape his will and affections and actions if he is to live the life of religion, of self-adaptation to the ultimate realities. Doubtless, as an expression, it is full of distortions, excesses, defects; its truth lies inextricably mixed with error as gold in the ore; yet the ore may be richer than any yet given to man; and pure gold may be unattainable as long as man is man. It is only through the variegated stained glass of some such creed that God's pure colourless light streams in upon us to guide us; it is only through the same that we can look upwards to the source of that light which we, perforce, clothe with these same forms and colours of the medium through which we view it. What we adore in Christ, what we reverence in Mary or in the Saints, is, in the last resort, God, the absolute Goodness; when we approach Christ as our Redeemer, or the Saints as our intercessors, it is God whom we approach. In itself an empty unfurnished conception, that of the absolute Goodness becomes furnished and defined when it stands for the source and fulness of all that wealth of love and goodness and spiritual beauty which is unfolded for us in the Catholic conceptions of the Incarnation, the Eucharist, the Sacred Heart, the Blessed Mother, the Saints, the Sacraments. Only through such conceptions can we draw nigh to God, or can He draw nigh to us, since we cannot see or conceive Him or deal with Him save as revealed in the finite. "Whatsoever ye did to the least of these, ye did unto Me" is the root-principle of the whole matter; we can worship and entertain Him unawares. Whatever we render to the goodness of the creature in the way of praise, reverence, or service passes straight on to the Creator regardless of our more limited intention; while He is not jealous when, without thought of Him, we ascribe to them the help that flows to us only from Him through their mediation. But though every determination of the creed, every new symbol of divine goodness given to us by the beliefs and worships of the faithful (where these are spiritual and true to the Gospel type), colour our conception of God more definitely and give a new tone to our sentiment towards Him, yet He is not for us a sum-total or generalization of such accumulated goodnesses, but their simple source, other and infinitely better than all. Their whole religious value lies in the modification they effect in our feeling towards Him as their author.

If then faith means entering into the Divine vision, looking out upon the whole with the eyes of God, being raised above the level of the natural understanding and faculties of calculation to a dim but more comprehensive view of reality, it is I think evident that this sort of vision is evoked, fostered, educated and determined by our association with the Catholic Church, of whose collective faith we are made heirs. Not as though an obedient appropriation of the Creed by our understanding were itself faith; but because it is an occasion and a criterion of faith. For as the Roman Communion is not coextensive with the whole of the spiritual world, with the Invisible Church, so neither is her creed, her collective mind and teaching, coextensive with the mind of the whole, with that Vision of which faith is a sharing—a vision that includes the creed as the vision of a single expanse of country might be said to include that of its military chart with all its divisions and subdivisions and complexities. Faith is not a sharing in the common creed of the visible Church, but in the common vision of the invisible Church which is, in a measure, that of God Himself.

Similarly in looking on the Roman Church as identical with that apostolic, missionary, and in some sense militant, body sent forth by Christ to preach and prepare the Kingdom of God; as a society devoted to the cause of religion upon earth; in devoting ourselves to its service, in throwing ourselves into its aims, we are taken out of our private littleness and begin to live with the full public life of that society, a life that is not in deed and in fact coextensive with that of the invisible Church, of the entire communion of souls bound together by the indwelling of the same divine spirit; but one which is included therein, as being organic thereto, as being an effectual, if not altogether indispensable,[10] sacrament of the same. Catholicism, if it stops short, is a narrower sentiment than divine charity, a poorer love both in scope and quality, yet it can waken, foster, direct, and embody that fuller spirit by which it is itself at once informed and transcended.

Once more, by our identification with this external society (so far as it is a vital and voluntary and not merely a mechanical and passive adhesion) our separate weakness is supplemented by a participation in its strength and resources; we are borne up by the crowd, carried along by its rush. Our convictions are stronger, our purposes firmer, our feelings are keener for being consciously shared by the whole world we live in. Our courage and hope and confidence are measured by our sense of the strength of the army to which we belong, of the history of its past victories. The Church's spiritual strength is not indeed coextensive with that infinite force of Divine Goodness which works within us and which we appropriate by the virtue of supernatural Hope; but it is an element in that strength, an instrument of its appropriation.

In all ways, then, communion with the visible Church is an effectual sacrament of communion with the invisible, a condition greatly favouring the supernatural life of Faith, Hope, and Charity.

But to come more to the concrete and practical;[11] putting aside all theological problems, you will still allow that for you the Crucifix represents the highest ideal of life; that Jesus stands for the most perfect type of humanity *in individuo;* that He is the central and supereminent figure round whose Cross are gathered the Christs of all ages, races, religions, and degrees, all those who like Him have believed the true value and purpose of life to lie in battling strenuously and self-unsparingly for the will of God, for truth and justice, for the redemption of man; who have realized that in this they were living a divine life of personal union with God, yielding themselves as instruments to a Divine Power that wrought in them and through them. You can still look on the individual "Christ-crucified" as the bond and centre of this collective mystical "Christ-crucified"; and you can desire to be incorporated with the same, to be on the side of the saints of humanity, canonized or uncanonized.

Dogma apart, and taken at its lowest, the Eucharist remains for you the sacrament of communion and incorporation with that mystical "Christ-crucified"; an act by which you offer yourself to be received into that divine company or spiritual organism, to be made a sharer of its faith, its hope and its love, to give your own body and blood "for many for the remission of sins."

Again in the Eucharistic chalice, mingled with the blood of Christ, you can still see the blood (that is, the sufferings, pains, and self-sacrifices) of all God's victims from the beginning; of those who in His cause have gone forth like Christ as sheep into the midst of wolves for the salvation of their blind persecutors; whose death and self-oblation is most precious in His eyes and constitutes the great sacrifice of praise and propitiation continually offered to God by the just of all ages "from the rising of the sun to the going down of the same"—the *Sacrificium justitiæ*, the sacrifice of "troubled spirits and of broken and contrite hearts." When you hear Mass you can still do so with a desire and intention of uniting your life in self-sacrifice with this endless, world-wide self-sacrifice of the mystical Christ for the same ends in the same spirit.

And if ever your conscience is seriously troubled, and you feel that you have cut yourself off from the spiritual unity of this mystical Christ, there is no reason why you should not still see in the sacrament of penance a means of reconciliation. Through it, as through the Eucharist and the other sacraments, the Invisible takes a tangible, manageable shape suited to our incorporate spirit and its modes of thought and action. The priest is the official representative not merely of God but more directly of that communion of the good in whom God is revealed, against which we have offended, with which we would be at peace.

It is plain to me that as I said "the truths by which you really live and grow are few and simple, and too fundamental to be involved in the fate of anything so contingent as a theological system; that even what is most characteristically Christian and Catholic in the lives of the greatest saints has but little dependence on the complexities of ecclesiastical teachings and ordinances, and as a fact obtained among the Apostles and Disciples of Christ generations before the said complexities were called into existence." If you are as good a Catholic as Simon Peter, I do not see why you need doubt your due loyalty to his successor. If you can live on the undeveloped germ, you may dispense with the developments, especially if they but puzzle and hinder you. For, after all, the visible Church (unlike the invisible) is but a means, a way, a creature, to be used where it helps, to be left where it hinders.[12] It is not the Kingdom of Heaven, but only its herald and servant. As I said before, we must allow for the class-interest of a priesthood that lives by the Altar, and not take its wares at the advertisement valuation; else we shall be in danger of denying them any value whatever.

After all, your quarrel is not with the Church, but with the theologians; not with ecclesiastical authority, but with a certain theory as to the nature and limits and grades of that authority, and of the value, interpretation and obligation of its decisions. A breakdown of theory and analysis does not do away with the reality analysed. You will say that authority has appropriated the theory and adopted the analysis; you will quote popes and councils and congregations and doctors in proof. But are you not begging the question? Who formulate these decisions, determine their value, interpret them to us; who have fabricated the whole present theology of authority and imposed it upon us, but the theologians? Who have taught us that the consensus of theologians cannot err, but the theologians themselves? Mortal, fallible, ignorant men like ourselves! Let us keep our heads cool, and not be terrified when they dress themselves up in the Church's robes and thunder their anathemas at us in her name. Their present domination is but a passing episode in the Church's history. Already their authority-theory is stretched to snapping-point, and self-strangled by inherent contradictions and preposterous consequences.

For the most part, theologians are as sincere and convinced of what they say as of old were many of those most faithful and observant Jews who would give no ear to Christ and His heresy; who quoted the Prophets to show that salvation was of the Jews alone, that Judaism would endure till the final Parousia and would at last conquer the whole world to its sway. How right they were and yet how wrong! Judaism was to live a risen and glorified life in Christianity. Paul did not feel that he had broken with Judaism, but that he had thrown down its barriers and opened it out into a world-religion, that he had but interpreted it. To the end he was a Hebrew of Hebrews; and we rightly boast ourselves to be the true, the spiritual Israel and seed of Abraham. Well, may not history repeat itself? May not theologians be right in quite another sense than they imagine? Is God's arm shortened that He should not again out of the very stones raise up seed to Abraham? May not Catholicism like Judaism have to die in order that it may live again in a greater and grander form? Has not every organism got its limits of development after which it must decay, and be content to survive in its progeny? Wine-skins stretch, but only within measure; for there comes at last a bursting-point when new ones must be provided.[13]

Who can answer these questions?

We can only turn the pages of history and wonder and wait.

Believe me,
With unaltered esteem and affection,
Yours faithfully,
G. TYRRELL, S.J.

NOTES

Note 1. Page 43

Here I was not speaking of Faith and Dogma, doubts as to which are settled by the ecumenical authority of the Church, with whom it rests to say what beliefs are involved in the revelation of Christ and in the life of the Christian people. Such decisions are in a sense doctrinal, yet they are not reached by, nor do they rest on, the reasonings which often accompany them. As implied in the life of Grace, they are ultimately the utterances of the Spirit from whom that life springs. They are authoritative in a sense which does not hold of the scientific conclusions of theologians. We do not therefore lack ecumenical authorities in dogma; but at present we lack theological experts competent to shape a scientific expression of revelation which shall be in harmony with current knowledge and modes of thought. To demand harmony between things of a totally different order, between prophetic and scientific truth, is absurd. But between scientific truth and the scientific expression of prophetic truth we have a right to demand harmony. The theology which cannot effect it is bankrupt.

Note 2. Page 44

It may be, and often is nowadays, objected that laymen have no business to meddle with theology at all; that it is by nature a clerical preserve; or that at all events none but the professional theologian, lay or cleric, should presume so high. But, for the first point, priest and theologian are surely not convertible terms; and it is a thing to regret that lay interest in religious questions is so long dead that a lay D.D. is as rare as a white crow. And for the second, I ask: Do the experts in any science work and write solely, even if principally, for their fellow-experts, and not rather for the edification of the educated world in general? Else how is the synthesis of sciences to be effected, if each body of experts forbids the members of other bodies to judge and criticize their labours? Every educated layman, without being a theological expert, ought to be interested in theology, and ought to be competent —more competent perhaps than a pure theologian—to criticize its bearings on knowledge in general, and certainly on any department of knowledge in which he himself happens to be an expert.

Note 3. Page 49

This is one of the passages quoted in the "Corriere della Sera" as particularly startling and scandalous; and certainly it is not the sort of thing one would care to say in the pulpit before a mixed congregation. If it now seems to me a lesser evil to publish it with an explanation than to withhold it, the responsibility rests with the correspondent of the journal in question, and still more with those whose action has given a monstrous notoriety to a document which must therefore be seen in order to be reduced to its proper dimensions. The shortest justification of what is here said would be found in the simple reproduction of the indictment which it epitomizes. But I have given my reason for refraining from that course even at the cost of weakening my own case. Clearly the indirect method of my reply demanded that, far from disputing the details of the said indictment, I should be ready to admit all and even more, and yet show the irrelevancy of the allegations. However eloquently presented, however richly documented and reinforced these charges were, yet in substance they were not, after all, so very original and startling as the "Corriere" seemed to think. Who is really ignorant nowadays of the difficulties raised by New Testament criticism, difficulties affecting not only details of faith, but the very rule of faith itself, both Scripture and Tradition? It is not for nothing that

A MUCH-ABUSED LETTER

Pope Leo XIII appointed his Biblical Commission. Or who is ignorant that the old assumptions as to the apostolic antiquity of many dogmatic and institutional forms are called in question by historical criticism? or that natural explanations are now offered to account for many wonders, or beliefs in wonders, once viewed as miraculous? Again, is not the high moral and religious character of multitudes outside the Church, the low attainments of multitudes inside, a continual, I do not say insuperable, problem for thoughtful and observant men? Is there any "note" of the true Church more difficult to deal with in theology than that of sanctity? Who, again, is unfamiliar with the shock experienced by the cultivated lay mind at first encounter with certain pages in ascetic and moral theology which I need not specify; or with the charge of enervating unwholesomeness often made against certain schools of spiritual direction? or with that against merely protective methods of moral education; or against secular principles introduced into spiritual government? I cannot see how any moderately instructed person can deny the existence of any one or all of these difficulties, or pretend to be scandalized at their bare enumeration. Most of them admit of a direct solution more or less satisfactory; but it was not my purpose to deal with them in detail, but rather to heap them up as high as possible, and say that all that and much more was simply irrelevant.

When I speak of the ultra-conservative scriptural positions being maintained only by systematic or else by involuntary ignorance—[the "Corriere" mistranslates this by "sistematica o voluntaria"—"systematic, or in other words voluntary"]— I designedly use the word "systematic" rather than "voluntary" because I know from my own past self-experiences, and from my long acquaintance and alliance with the conservative school, that what would be subjectively dishonest for one who admits the principle of free inquiry is subjectively honest and morally obligatory for one who does not. It is simply part of his system of authority. Of course, on both sides there are plenty of bigots and unfair controversialists. But besides those who *will* not inquire through lack of candour, there are, on the conservative side, those who, as a matter of principle and conscience, *will* not read, or permit those under them to read, what might shake the foundations of their moral and spiritual life; who find in that life itself an indirect but forcible argument for all those beliefs on which it depends, and one which exempts them—as any truly sufficient argument ought to—from further inquiry. Though I am not for unqualified pragmatism, I have too much sympathy with its dominant idea to be blind to the merits of this conservative position. Life, even in its deepest and widest sense, may not be the sole test of truth; but it is perhaps the most important.

Note 4. Page 52

The correspondent of the "Corriere" will not be alone in regarding my practical conclusion and advice as strange and audacious. He will have for company all those who know nothing whatever about the ordinary practice of prudent confessors and directors in dealing with such cases. Of late years the problem of conformity has become a pressing one with multitudes of the educated and modern-minded laity of both sexes, and every fashionable confessor has to deal with it daily; and I venture to say that in nine cases out of ten he differs from me only in obeying a confused instinct instead of a clear principle; that his advice is the same and that his implicit reasons are the same. In theory he may be an "intellectualist," he may not distinguish theological difficulties from doubts against faith; but his spiritual instinct is better than his theory, and at a sacrifice of consistency he will usually advise an obviously devout and sincere penitent to go on practising his religion, in spite of his so-called "doubts against faith." He will perhaps call these theological doubts "scruples"; or refuse to believe that the penitent has "consented" to them—somewhat to the bewilderment of the latter.

The old-fashioned or unfashionable confessor is a much more consistent "intellectualist," and by no means suffers the reasons of the heart to plead against those of the head. For him, Revelation being a divinely authorized theology, he does

A MUCH-ABUSED LETTER

not seem to himself free to make any concessions. The penitent must take it as a whole or leave it. He may wisely lock it away in a corner of his brain and not attempt to harmonize it with the rest of his thought; but if he makes that attempt everything must make way for this divine theology; everything must be thrown out and denied that conflicts with it. Such direction is much easier for the confessor; much less confusing for the penitent. Unfortunately it would quickly weed out of the Church thousands of her most intelligently devoted children than whom none have a better right to her sacraments and ministrations; and who are in some sense the harbingers of a more vigorous future that perhaps may be in front of her.

Note 5. Page 54

In supposing that I have hit on a new idea in this distinction between the consciousness and subconsciousness of the Church or any other Society, the correspondent of the "Corriere" credits me with greater originality than I possess. Perhaps if I had spoken instead of the explicit and implicit mind of the Church, he might have recognized the distinction as venerable with the weight of centuries. It has played no small part surely in the controversy between the more progressive Roman Church and those less progressive Oriental communions to whom it was ever answered that alleged innovations had really pre-existed from the beginning in the implicit mind—that is to say, in the subconsciousness of the Church. Even the most conservative theory of doctrinal development involves the distinction in question. Else it would be impossible to defend not only particular dogmas like the Immaculate Conception, ignored by saints and doctors in the past, from the charge of novelty, but still more a dogma like the Papal Infallibility touching the very rule of faith itself. How can the defenders of that dogma deny that the Church grows in self-understanding, or that in earlier days she did not know, consciously and explicitly, what she was; but only so far as this knowledge was latent and potential in the living organism? After all, what could be more fundamentally important than the precise place and function of the Pope in the constitution of the Church? Yet for two thousand years the point was obscure and disputed. Even still how much remains vague as to the exact quality, extent, limits, conditions of papal and sub-papal authority! What has been, may be; and in this case must be. The very condition of such growth and progress is that in every age there are some who intuitively read and interpret the subconsciousness of the Church better than others, and who therefore realize the comparative inadequacy of her explicit self-expression. Else there had been no Vatican Council. It is therefore altogether inept to brand with the infamous note of originality a distinction so commonplace and inevitable.

Note 6. Page 55

Here, and in parallel passages, it is impossible to deny that the expression is "theologically" defensible only in virtue of a decidedly "non-natural" reading and distinction. As it stands, it is not only offensive to received theology, it is also untrue to the principle of which it pretends to be the application; nor does it rightly represent either the difficulty in question or the solution. It errs by accepting an inaccurately stated objection and by replying in the same inaccurate terms. It falls into the slipshod usage which confounds the Church with Churchmen, with her theological exponents and apologists. What is meant is perfectly sound, and was so taken by the questioner. What is said is theologically unsound, since the explanatory context is absent.

The Church's self-utterance is twofold. At rare times she is stirred to her very depths and throughout her whole frame; and the buried thoughts of her heart find expression in what is truly and properly an ecumenical utterance forced from her by the necessities of her corporate life, and as it were under pain of extinction. From the very nature of the case these utterances are the spontaneous expression of her buried self. They are not exhaustive, but they cannot but be faithful. But in her silent intervals theology proceeds with its analysis and deductions to conclusions forced on it merely by the laws of thought,

A MUCH-ABUSED LETTER

not by the necessities of the Church's spiritual life. The schools have no special charisma; they are no integral part of the teaching Church, yet they are allowed to speak for the Church, subject always to those ecumenical utterances which, as revealing her deeper and universal mind, are alone truly hers.

It is precisely (as indeed the whole trend of my Letter makes evident) the schools that were in question, and that scholastic presentment of the Church found in current manuals and larger catechisms, and forced upon my correspondent by a somewhat intransigent confessor. These are to the Church what a dominant political party may be to the country. They strive to represent its mind, but they may fail, and may have to "go to the country" on some question or another. No one disputes the verdict of the whole country in such a case; but prior to such an appeal one may well dispute the fidelity of any particular party to the sense of the country. That seems to me the attitude one might take with regard to the teaching of the schools and, to some extent, of non-ecumenical and reversible decisions of all kinds. We may have a deep immovable faith in the unformulated sense of the Church at large, and yet very little confidence in the dominant school of interpretation, in those who are allowed to speak for the Church till such time as she herself shall speak.

Note 7. Page 59

Not merely is the class in question an important and necessary element in the Church's constitution, but its seeming egotism and self-assertiveness is no matter for surprise or scandal. We have studies nowadays of the psychology of crowds, classes, and peoples; we need as urgently a study of the ethics of such collective entities. Too much mischief has been done by a fallacy of personification which subjects a class or corporate body to the same code of morality as the individual; which overlooks its almost entirely non-moral, law-determined nature. The self-assertiveness of classes and interests, the effort of each to be first and sole, is as necessary for the healthy and vigorous development of State or Church as the unchecked fulfilment of that desire in any one case would be detrimental, or even fatal, to that general balance of contending interests which constitutes the health of a community. The charge of egotism against an individual might be scandalous; against a class it is indifferent, or, rather, meaningless.

Note 8. Page 62

Plainly, what I mean by this too elliptical expression is that nearly every schism has been the work of the worst men on both sides, who have prevented the best from coming to an understanding. When I say "the Church" I mean the Churchmen. He would be a hardy controversialist who should maintain that the Protestant Reformation was in no way accountable to the ecclesiastics of the Renaissance.

Note 9. Page 69

In religion as in other departments of our spirit-life we need social tradition to rouse and shape the growth of our faculties. The Church's teaching is normally requisite to elicit our faith. As hearsay evidence it can win our intellectual assent. But we do not hold it as God's word, or by faith, except in virtue of an act of intuition, a response of spirit to spirit, a recognition of a voice heard before.

Note 10. Page 82

This expression ought not to need much apology nowadays. I cannot but suspect that the saying, *Extra ecclesiam salus nulla* (No safety outside the Church), with its evident allusion to the ark of Noah, comes down to us from the time when "the Communion of Saints" was taken in apposition as a synonym for "the Holy Catholic Church." Of that invisible Catholic Church or Communion of Saints it is true as of Noah's ark that all inside are saved; all outside, lost. But when transferred to the visible Church the saying is doubly pointless, since, as every theologian allows, all inside that ark are not saved; all outside it are not lost. Still, communion with that society may be a normally, if not absolutely, necessary condition of safety, albeit by no means a sufficient guarantee.

Note 11. Page 83

I hope it is obvious, though I am afraid it is not, that to insist as I do here on the lower and humbler values of the Church and her dogmas and ordinances is not to deny or

A MUCH-ABUSED LETTER

belittle the higher values. Believing my correspondent to be in absolutely good faith, and to have the hidden roots of his religion sound and healthy; knowing that what ails him is no real loss of faith, but merely theological bewilderment; my whole purpose is to put his soul into movement and exercise; to get him to live vigorously according to such light as still remains to him; to show him that the paralysis produced by his doubts is at most partial, and need by no means bring his practical religious life to that standstill which might really result in a torpor of the heart and affections, and thus in a decay of the root of recovery.

Obviously, it is in respect to their "all-or-nothing" principle that I differ most fundamentally in mind and sentiment from the intransigent school—if indeed it be, as I hope, only a school. Thus, I would infinitely rather see a Catholic country protestantized than de-Christianized; I would rather see it de-Christianized than bereft of all religion. Nothing could persuade me that it was right to prefer a greater risk of the greater evil, to a lesser risk of the lesser. And so as to individuals; if I cannot get all, I will be thankful for a half or a quarter. If this be a heresy it is His who has taught us not to despise the day of small things, nor to break the bruised reed, nor to quench the smoking flax, and who was not altogether grateful to the zealots who would drive from His blessing and embrace those who, however immature, were their co-heirs in the Kingdom of Heaven.

Note 12. Page 86

This is ambiguous; but defensible even in the unintended sense. For, after all, there are rare occasions when communion with the visible Church can be maintained only at cost of principle; occasions when saints have had to choose between the one and only absolute duty and the highest sort of conditional duty. It is a Pope who has said: "A man should bear excommunication rather than sin mortally"; nor may we suppose he would allow one to sin venially or to admit the slightest moral evil in order to escape such a catastrophe; and again: "No man should act against his conscience, but should follow his conscience rather than the injunction [sententiam] of the Church in a case where he feels certain" (quoted in "Historisch-politische Blätter," p. 427, München, 1900). Yet here I do not speak of communion with the Church, which I am insisting on at all costs; but of the immense variety of means which she offers for our help—some for the use of all; all for the use of none.

Note 13. Page 89

It might be objected by a theologian that this last paragraph seems to imply the possibility of as radical a revolution in the constitution of the Church as that by which Judaism was transformed into Christianity. This, moreover, sounds perilously like admitting the possibility of a new dispensation such as that which was expected by the disciples of Abbot Joachim and other medieval fanatics. Yet it cannot be denied that on the surface, at least, there was far less difference between Judaism and the Christianity of S. James' espistle than between the latter and the Catholicism of Gregory VII. There is no assignable reason why the future should not witness as great or even greater transformations consistent with substantial identity of the body so transformed. The differences between the larval and final stages of many an insect are often far greater and more startling than those which separate kind from kind. The Church of the Catacombs became the Church of the Vatican; who can tell what the Church of the Vatican may not turn into?

And then, with all deference to the correspondent of the "Corriere," it does not strike me as altogether uncomplimentary to the theologians to credit them with a certain prophetic faculty of uttering more and not less than they are distinctly aware of; or to imply that what they say of the Church and her authority may be true in a far higher sense and degree than they quite suspect. I know they are commonly credited with claiming the crudest sort of finality and exhaustiveness for their theories; but I feel sure that their faith in the Church cannot be so thin and cold as to allow the best of them to imagine that they have compassed all she is and may be.

EPILOGUE

I HAVE now perhaps said enough to show that there are few if any passages in the Letter for which it is not possible to make out some kind of theological defence even though its avowed purpose is, not indeed to assail theology, but to thrust it down to its proper place at the footstool of Faith. If my justification in writing it is not quite evident to the reader in default of full acquaintance with the circumstances and difficulties of my correspondent, to me it is abundantly evident, and I have no hesitation on the subject whatever. Nor do I feel very guilty so far as I frequently applied the same plaster to what I myself judged to be approximately the same sort of wounds. One cannot fabricate such letters every other day for each new comer. It was perhaps less exquisitely prudent to commit its private distribution to the judgment of others; yet it seemed that the risk of harm was slight compared with the probability of benefit. To complain of those I trusted would be unjust and ungenerous. If they were too confiding the fault lies not with them, but with their confidants.

But if there is a fair case for me, there is perhaps as fair a one for the other side.

In the first place the Letter, though implicitly quite respectful to theology, is not at all calculated to propitiate those theologians who are really at the bottom of the opposition to it. If a sin against theology is bad, a sin against the theologians is worse. Better trouble the stream than the fountain. One may quite lawfully and charitably pass criticisms on the absent which, brought to their ears, would most reasonably rouse their resentment. Can one expect to be leniently judged by theologians who in his private correspondence has been discovered speaking but moderately of their craft; suggesting that they should not be taken too seriously; that they have been negligent in their accounts; that they are threatened with bankruptcy; and, worst of all, that such bankruptcy would leave God in His Heaven as undisturbed as were the stars by the bankruptcy of the Ptolemaic astronomy? What kind of judgment would a committee of old-fashioned physicians pass on a hygienic treatise that spoke in similar terms of drugs and doctors?

Again, though it was never destined for miscellaneous circulation, and as such cannot merit the censures proper to such documents, yet as a fact it was made public by the notice in the "Corriere" which, in spite of the ineptitude of the citations adduced in proof, branded it as the extremest extant utterance of Liberal Catholicism.

Again, popes, black and white, are by no means free agents to the extent commonly supposed. The interest and the characteristic policy of an institution must be maintained at the expense of any individual member. That what was said to be the extremest utterance of liberalism should proceed from that Order which stands for the extremest anti-liberalism was a somewhat intolerable anomaly that called for instant remedy. A prolix justification of the Letter such as I have attempted here might have satisfied a reflective few, but would not have erased the sensational effect of the "scandal" with the many. Hence, though I could not honestly comply with the order of unqualified repudiation, yet I hardly see, from a governmental point of view, what other order could have been given. When dignitaries are scandalized, and the souls of cardinals imperilled, something must be done at once, nor is there time for the niceties of ideal justice.

For these and many other reasons that I might allege, I cannot feel all that burning and unqualified indignation against my opponents which so many of my friends feel in my behalf. In early life one is surprised and aggrieved at opposition. One sees clear to the horizon in every direction. As one advances, what seemed mere cloud-banks solidify into mountain ranges towering up into impassable snow-capped barriers. One no longer expects to walk through; and if one is worsted in attempting to cross, one takes one's falls and broken bones as part of the game, and begins again as soon as possible.

If, then, I now make public what was at first meant and suited only for very narrow circulation, I do so reluctantly, and solely because under all the altered circumstances I am convinced that such a course will remove far more scandal than it may cause. I do it on my own responsibility; advised by nobody; dissuaded by many. I do it as a duty to others; above all as a duty to my own conscience, from which no one can dispense me.

G. T.

20 *September*, 1906.

www.ingramcontent.com/pod-product-compliance
Lightning Source LLC
LaVergne TN
LVHW021550080426
835510LV00019B/2465